BRO CODE DAILY DEVOTIONAL

NO NONSENSE PRAYER AND MOTIVATION
FOR MEN

SCOTT SILVERII

 Five
Stones
University

Five Stones Press /

Dallas, Texas, 75115

https://scottsilverii.com/bro-code-series/

Contact: Five Stones Press

contact@bluemarriage.com

All Scripture quotations, unless otherwise indicated, are taken from the New American Standard Bible, by The Lockman Foundation. Used by permission.

Other versions used are:

KJV—King James Version. Authorized King James Version.

NIV—Scripture taken from the Holy Bible, New International Version®. Used by permission of Zondervan Publishing House. All rights reserved.

Ordering Information:

Quantity sales. Special discounts will be made available on quantity purchases by corporations, associations, and others. For details, contact the publisher at the address above.

Printed in the United States of America

A title of a book : a subtitle of the same book / Bro Code Daily Devotional: No Nonsense Prayers and Motivation; Dr. Scott Silverii

1. The main category of the book —Spiritual Healing —Other category - PTSD. 2. Another subject category —Religious, Men's Health. 3. More categories — Psychology, Pain and Addiction.

HF0000.A0 A00 2010

14 13 12 11 10 / 10 9 8 7 6 5 4 3 2 1

DEDICATION

To the first, ultimate and only Alpha -
our Lord and Savior, Jesus Christ

INTRODUCTION

Instructions?

Yeah, I'm not a big fan of instructions either, but I want you to get the full benefit of this experience. Its simple - MAKE the time to read each day's prayer, scripture, and write out the Man Up and Pray Up sections.

There's space to write, draw, or do mathematical formulas. I don't like those either. But, the point is, we Bros are visual and hands-on & this book gives you room to roam.

Take advantage of it, and do more than read this if you remember where you left it. Be active and change your life over the next 31 days.

Either you paid for it, or someone who loves you bought it for you. Don't waste money or time! Make a commitment and work through this entire journal. I promise that the more you read, pray and write; the more you will benefit from it.

I have prayed over every day of this adventure and I know the words will speak to your soul because they aren't my words, they belong to God. I'm praying over you.

Much Love & Respect,
Scott

Let's Roll

Dear Warrior In Christ,

One of the most powerful moments in my life was when someone laid their hands on me in church, and I heard them begin to pray out loud for me.

The heat in my body rose, and I felt pure energy radiating through me. While both feet were bolted to the floor, my spirit soared at the words my brother spoke over me.

I believe in the power of prayer. I also believe in the God-ordained submission of men praying for each other. Even as a Chief of Police, I would stop what I was doing to pray for brothers in need as the Lord moved me.

That's what this devotional is all about. Each day I asked God to move in me through the Holy Spirit to give me words for various areas in your life. Every day, God placed a very specific word on my heart that I wrote to be shared with you.

I'm not a professional pastor, nor do I speak eloquently, but when I pray, I know my words hold the power of our almighty God, and that His messages are meant for warriors like you.

Much Love & Respect,
Scott

Day 1 Prayer

Lord God,

Sin shackles us to hell. Confession is our key to freedom. Lord, show our brothers that the way to cleanse their burdens is through confession.

Teach our brothers confession is not weakness, but strength through submission to You. I pray our brothers lean upon Your promise in 1 John 1:9. I pray this day for men to become like the mighty men of old. Men who delighted in Your presence, who treasured their wife, and committed completely to their children.

Show our brothers that redemption will never be found in work, no matter how hard they toil, but in the peace of surrender.

Amen

Bro Code Devotional

"If we confess our sins, He is faithful and just and will forgive us our sins and purify us from all unrighteousness."

1 John 1:9

Brotherly Advice

"There is one rule, above all others, for being a man. Whatever comes, face it on your feet."

— Robert Jordan

Man Up

This is your private prayer journal. Write the name of one person you hold a grudge against. You must forgive this person so that you will know freedom from their offense. Start with their name and write what you'd say to them.

Pray Up

Write your own prayer for today. It may be for your wife, kids, or yourself. Whatever God lays on your heart, write it out as a prayer.

Lord God,

I pray for our brothers who have allowed other gods to come before You. Maybe it's sports, hunting, partying, their wife, or kids. Lord, show them that anything, no matter what it is or how helpful it might be, is to take a backseat to You.

If it's a god much worse than listed above, I ask that You show our brothers the way to healing. Lord, too many brothers are trapped by their lust in addictions, adultery, and sexual sin. Help them, Father, to see how destructive these obsessions are.

They not only steal the light away from You, but they bury men even farther into slavery. Help our brothers understand that by focusing on You, that You shall care and provide for the rest. I thank You for Your words in Exodus 20:3 and Deuteronomy 5:7.

Amen

Bro Code Devotional

Thou shalt have no other gods before me.
Exodus 20:3
&
Deuteronomy 5:7

This is your private prayer journal. Write out the name of one person that you want forgiveness from. Then write out what you did to offend them, and a plea to Christ for forgiveness.

Pray Up

Write your own prayer for today. It may be for your wife, kids, or yourself. Whatever God lays on your heart, write it out as a prayer.

Lord Father,

My heart breaks for brothers who suffer from feelings of loneliness. Our sisters are so much better at meeting and making true friendships, that we men are often left alone, feeling unloved.

I pray that our brothers drop the hard shell and make themselves approachable to other brothers so that the Holy Spirit can introduce them to each other. The darkness of loneliness can become suffocating, but still brothers cling to their pride.

Father, show them there are many others in the same circumstance praying to escape the crush of solitude. You did not make us to be alone. Whether it is a friend or a co-worker, men naturally seek bonding with other men. This is how early man survived—by creating tribes, villages and communities. Lord, I pray they know they are not alone.

Amen

Bro Code Devotional

"And though one can overpower him who is alone, two can resist him. A cord of three strands is not quickly broken."
~ Ecclesiastes 4:12

Brotherly Advice

There are two questions a man has to ask:
The first is. 'Where am I going?' and the second is, 'Who will go with
me?' If you ever get these questions in the wrong order you are in
trouble."
— Sam Keen

Man Up

This is your private prayer journal. Write down the name of one person who was a positive force in your life. Then write out what you'd like to day to them.

Pray Up

Write your own prayer for today. It may be for your wife, kids, or yourself. Whatever God lays on your heart, write it out as a prayer.

Day 4 Prayer

Lord God,

You've placed the word covetousness on my heart to share with our brothers. We lose sight of the many blessings You give because we're too busy drooling over what the neighbor has, or what some celebrity on TV is driving, or what an athlete is wearing.

I pray that they turn their eyes from others and lift their hearts to You. That they shall see how amazingly giving You are.

Blessings are often where we seek them. If a brother is reading this, then having the liberty of being free to worship is just one of many blessings You provide.

Covetousness also places the desired item above their love for You. I pray nothing interferes with their heavenly line of sight.

Amen

"You shall not covet your neighbor's house. You shall not covet your neighbor's wife, or his male or female servant, his ox or donkey, or anything that belongs to your neighbor."
Exodus 20:17

Man Up

This is your private prayer journal. This is going to hurt, but you've got to expose pain to light for healing. Write down the ten worst things that happened to you since your youth.

Pray Up

Write your own prayer for today. It may be for your wife, kids, or yourself. Whatever God lays on your heart, write it out as a prayer.

Day 5 Prayer

Dear Lord,

I pray that You show our brothers how to deal with the anger that rages in their hearts. It is not a sin to be angry, but it is a sin to sin for the sake of anger. Anger is a human emotion that You blessed us with.

I pray that brothers do not allow it to control them, or to destroy them. If we have sinned against someone, please ask forgiveness. If someone has sinned against you and you are angry, forgive them.

Allow brothers to understand that forgiveness isn't about accepting the other's actions, it's about freeing themselves from the anger caused by the offense. Paul also reminds us in Ephesians that although we do get angry, that we are not to let the sun go down while still mad.

Amen

Bro Code Devotional

Be you angry, and sin not: let not the sun go down on your wrath"
Ephesians 4:26

Brotherly Advice

"Men, you'll never be a good groom to your wife unless you're first a good bride to Jesus."
— Timothy J. Keller

Man Up

This is your private prayer journal. Write down the name of one friend who you wish you'd been a better friend to. Then write what it was that prevented you from being that better friend.

Pray Up

Write your own prayer for today. It may be for your wife, kids, or yourself. Whatever God lays on your heart, write it out as a prayer.

Lord Father,

I pray for dads struggling over relationships with their children. You made parents to be Your image bearer. The young ones were meant to grow up to know You by watching and learning from their parents.

It seems so simple, but because man's separation from You through sin, this relationship is rarely simple. Our children's rejection is like a knife to our heart, and it covers dads with darkness. We dads carry so much guilt over strained and lost relationships that we often suffer the regrets for having condemned our kids to the potential cycle of generational sin we have experienced, because of strained relationships with our own dads.

Lord, I pray our brothers do not beat themselves up over the mistakes in parenting. I thank You for forgiving and restoring us so that we may continue to be present and active in their lives.

Amen

Bro Code Devotional

"He will restore the hearts of the fathers to their children and the hearts of the children to their fathers, so that I will not come and smite the land with a curse."

Malachi 4:6

This is your private prayer journal. This is the time for you to write out at least one more thing that you need to get off of your chest. Don't pull punches with God. It's time to dig deep and seek His will for your life.

Pray Up

Write your own prayer for today. It may be for your wife, kids, or yourself. Whatever God lays on your heart, write it out as a prayer.

Lord God,

I'm asking You for reconciliation for Brothers struggling in a marriage. You created marriage to reflect the intimate relationship we are to share with You. Your first miracle with man was the creation of woman and their union.

Jesus confirmed the value of marriage when His very first miracle was at a wedding. Revelations ends with the marriage supper. I pray for Brothers who are unsure or flat worn out over what to do to gain clarity to see the path You have set for them. Father, if they've sinned, please help them to understand the power of confession and the grace of forgiveness.

Lord, I know the devil hates marriage, and he's working overtime to rip them apart. I pray in the name of Jesus Christ for supernatural protection for our Brothers while they clear the path toward reconciling with their wives.

Amen

Bro Code Devotional

Be kind to one another, tenderhearted, forgiving one another, as God in Christ forgave you.
Ephesians 4:32

Brotherly Advice

"A man should be able to hear, and to bear, the worst that could be
said of him."
— Saul Bellow

Man Up

This is your private prayer journal. Write out your most favorite memory with your dad.

Pray Up

Write your own prayer for today. It may be for your wife, kids, or yourself. Whatever God lays on your heart, write it out as a prayer.

Day 8 Prayer

Dear Father,

I pray for finances. So many brothers are worried or consumed by finances. It's half way through the month and they're anxious about making it the rest of the way. Lord, this is satan working to shake their foundation.

You want an abundant life for us and promised to meet our needs. I know this doesn't mean to make a shopping wish list, but You want our brothers to seek Your will for their life. You will provide for the desires placed in their hearts. Father, I pray that our brothers hold faithful and learn to increase by giving away.

This begins with tithing 10%. It's not about giving money to a church, it's about being obedient to Your word. You do more when we do less. I pray a special blessing of peace over our brothers. Grant them an opportunity to experience the joy of life without the worry of paying bills.

Amen

Give, and it will be given to you. Good measure, pressed down, shaken together, running over, will be put into your lap. For with the measure you use it will be measured back to you."
Luke 6:38

Man Up

This is your private prayer journal. Write out how you feel about your mom, and how the job she did raising you.

Pray Up

Write your own prayer for today. It may be for your wife, kids, or yourself. Whatever God lays on your heart, write it out as a prayer.

Day 9 Prayer

Holy Father,

I pray for brothers struggling in their marriage or going through a divorce. You created the marriage covenant, and I pray they understand the significance of that eternal oath.

Genesis 2:25 "Therefore, a man shall leave his father and his mother and hold fast to his wife, and they shall become one flesh."

Father, You knew that it was not good for man to be alone (Genesis 2:18) so You created woman to be joined with man and even brought her to him (Genesis 2:22). In the first marriage ceremony in history, You said,

"a man shall leave his father and his mother and hold fast to his wife, and they shall become one flesh" (Genesis 2:24).

This holy matrimony uses language that typifies what it means to become husband and wife. The two become "one flesh," meaning that they are so unified that they actually become one.

They become one in unity, one in essence (as in family), one in purpose, and one in mind. The meaning of joined is like that of a bonding agent—like glue. This "joining" is so strong that it is like one part of the other will be ripped away from the other if they are ever separated.

If you joined two pieces of paper with glue and tore them apart, each sheet of paper would take with it part of the other. This is a great image of what divorce does. It damages both parties so much that both are hurt in the process, therefore they should cleave and not leave, because what You have joined together, no one should try to separate."

Amen

"Therefore, a man shall leave his father and his mother and hold fast to his wife, and they shall become one flesh."
Genesis 2:25

Brotherly Advice

A man's ledger does not tell what he is, or what he is worth. Count what is in man, not what is on him, if you would know what he is worth—whether rich or poor.
–Henry Ward Beecher

Man Up

This is your private prayer journal. Write out three things you wish you hadn't done in the last 10 years and what were their consequences.

Pray Up

Write your own prayer for today. It may be for your wife, kids, or yourself. Whatever God lays on your heart, write it out as a prayer.

Day 10 Prayer

Holy Father,

Today You have placed the burden of infidelity on my heart. Lord, I pray for our brothers who battle the flesh. Father, I said the burden of infidelity instead of saying the sin of infidelity because our brothers understand it is a grave sin, but most do not understand that it is a burden.

Many brothers who act out sexually do not know why they do so. Many promise to behave and be loyal, and in their hearts they truly do wish to be faithful. But the chains of satan's temptation to pursue the flesh is more powerful than our brothers' will to flee.

This, my Lord is their burden, which causes their sin. Brothers continue to relive this act of defiance, oath-breaking, and covetousness each time they flirt, text, bait-click pornography, steal a simple kiss at the after work happy-hour, or commit to long-term or repeated sexual affairs.

I pray that they seek Your will to delete, erase, or block women who they hide from their wife on social media or texting. Help them know the joy of marital purity by busting those chains that drag them down through sexual sin.

Amen

Flee from sexual immorality. Every other sin a person commits is outside the body, but the sexually immoral person sins against his own body.
1 Corinthians 6:18

Man Up

This is your private prayer journal. Write out the name of one person who caused you grief as a child. Then explain how that makes you feel still today.

Pray Up

Write your own prayer for today. It may be for your wife, kids, or yourself. Whatever God lays on your heart, write it out as a prayer.

Dear Father,

I pray for brothers who have hurt someone they loved and are now struggling with not asking for forgiveness. I also pray that they gain a clear understanding of what forgiveness means. Too often people refuse to forgive others.

God, You are very clear that if we do not forgive others, that You will not forgive us. I pray that our brothers humble themselves before those they have wronged by asking them to forgive them. Please show our brothers that being forgiven also does not mean the hurtful action has been forgotten.

Many times brothers ask for prayer that their spouse returns and that they have changed. Too often these brothers expect their wife to forgive and forget what they did to hurt them. While they may forgive, it may require time and patience for the trust to return. This, my Lord, is where many brothers get impatient and turn against their wives because she may still be struggling with the offense that first hurt them.

Father, I pray that our brothers learn to say, "I'm sorry," and "Please forgive me." When they cause pain through their actions. I pray that they truly repent and see the wrong that they do and the damage that they cause.

I pray that You soften the hardness of their hearts, and allow them to know what being forgiven really feels like. It was You that forgave us of our sins, and You that allowed Your Son to die because of our sins. We praise You for the gift of grace and salvation.

Amen

Bro Code Devotional

Therefore, confess your sins to one another and pray for one another, that you may be healed. The prayer of a righteous person has great power as it is working.
James 5:16

Brotherly Advice

"We do not admire the man of timid peace. We admire the man who embodies victorious effort; the man who never wrongs his neighbor, who is prompt to help a friend, but who has those virile qualities necessary to win in the stern strife of actual life."
–Theodore Roosevelt

Man Up

This is your private prayer journal. Write out two regrets in your life. Then explain how they affected your life at the time, and now.

Pray Up

Write your own prayer for today. It may be for your wife, kids, or yourself. Whatever God lays on your heart, write it out as a prayer.

Holy Lord,

I pray for mercy received and mercy shown. You placed the message of mercy on my heart to be shared with our brothers. Mercy is when we deserve to be punished because of our sin, but instead, we are spared the punishment by You, Lord.

I pray our brothers understand how often Your judgment is deserved because of our actions, but by Your mercy, we are spared. Father, with this in mind, I pray that our brothers also show mercy to those within their power to punish or discipline.

It's easy to withhold something of value or swing a hand to harm another, but it is by Your example of sparing us when we deserve destruction, that I pray our brothers abide. True strength comes from showing mercy and mentoring the offending person toward the right path. Any bully can strike, but a true Christian brother will show mercy.

Amen

So speak and so act as those who are to be judged under the law of liberty. For judgment is without mercy to one who has shown no mercy. Mercy triumphs over judgment.
James 2:12-13

Man Up

This is your private prayer journal. This is the time for you to write out another thing that you need to get off of your chest. Don't pull punches with God, it's time to dig deep and seek His will for your life.

Pray Up

Write your own prayer for today. It may be for your wife, kids, or yourself. Whatever God lays on your heart, write it out as a prayer.

Day 13 Prayer

Dear Father,

As I sit across from my wife, I'm moved to pray for Godly women. I pray our brothers understand the eternal value of having a woman in their life who loves You first, Lord.

Father, I pray for women who seek Your heart with all of theirs. Church pews are filled with these virtuous women, yet too often they go unnoticed and unappreciated by the very men they are praying for. Father, I pray for these women.

I ask You to bless them for their faithfulness. Lord please allow them to always know they are loved, respected and protected by our brothers. Allow them to see Your face in the midst of their burdens for family. Show these blessed women that they truly are as Solomon said in Proverbs far above rubies.

Amen

"Who can find a virtuous woman? for her price is far above rubies."
Proverbs 31:10

Brotherly Advice

"Relieved of moral pretense and stripped of folk costumes, the raw masculinity that all men know in their gut has to do with being good at being a man within a small, embattled gang of men struggling to survive."

–Jack Donovan

This is your private prayer journal. Write out how your last signifi-cant relationship ended and why. Also, what would you have done better.

Pray Up

Write your own prayer for today. It may be for your wife, kids, or yourself. Whatever God lays on your heart, write it out as a prayer.

Dear Lord,

I pray our brothers know how blessed and loved they are. No matter what obstacle are in their paths, or the worries that occupy their mind, I ask You to open their eyes and ears to know they are covered by the blood of Your Son, Jesus Christ.

No matter how bad they screwed up in life, that they do not get to control the story that You have written for them. I pray they come to know You, and trust that You have a plan for them. That they realize their life was not an accident, Each day shouldn't be lived only because they happened to wake up.

Our brothers are prayed for every day by us and they should see the Godly women who also lift them up. God, I beg that our brothers see they are no failure. That they can turn their stories around by turning them over to You. I pray our brothers feel the love and respect we give them in daily prayers. Let us pray without ceasing for our brothers to be the real, old-school men of men.

Amen

Bro Code Devotional

"Rejoice always, pray without ceasing, in everything give thanks; for this is the will of God in Christ Jesus for you."
1Thessalonians 5:16-18

This is your private prayer journal. Write about the first time you realized there was a God, and how your relationship with Him has progressed.

Pray Up

Write your own prayer for today. It may be for your wife, kids, or yourself. Whatever God lays on your heart, write it out as a prayer.

Dear Lord,

I pray that we look at each other as our brother's keeper. I know the line is attributed to Cain when he killed Abel, but there are many references in Your word to one brother looking out after the other. I love Matthew 25:35

"For I was hungry and you gave me food, I was thirsty and you gave me drink, I was a stranger and you welcomed me"

Father, I know following you isn't for wimps. You called us to be men and to expect tough times because we love You. You said we will be persecuted for Your name's sake, but that we would be blessed.

Dear Father, I pray a blessing for these brothers because they have taken a stand for You, and they have stood among one another as their brother's friend and keeper.

Amen

Bro Code Devotional

"Blessed are you when people insult you and persecute you, and falsely say all kinds of evil against you because of Me.
~ Matthew 5:11

Brotherly Advice

"We don't need to reinvent manliness. We only need to will ourselves to wake up from the bad dream of the last few generations and reclaim it, in order to extend and enrich that tradition under the formidable demands of the present."
–Waller R. Newell

Man Up

This is your private prayer journal. Write out about how you feel you handle money and finances. Are you financially secure. If not, what do you need to change in your behavior.

Pray Up

Write your own prayer for today. It may be for your wife, kids, or yourself. Whatever God lays on your heart, write it out as a prayer.

Dear Lord,

I am so thankful for my wife and our marriage. She and our marriage are gifts, and I value it because I love the Gift Giver –You. You know I've not always acted to show my love, and I thank You for Your grace.

Our marriage endures because of our covenant with You. Father, I pray for our married brothers to see the significance of their own covenants between their wives and You. Father, show our brothers the power of a covenant, and that it is not a simple "contract" that can be broken.

Lord, show our brothers that while a contract generally has a term limit, covenants are eternal. Contracts are designed as a way for both parties to "get" something, covenants are filled by Your grace. Contracts deal with an "if...then" mentality.

The first step to divorce-proofing their marriage is to stop thinking of their union as an "if...then," and start thinking in terms of eternity.

Amen

However, let each one of you love his wife as himself, and let the wife see that she respects her husband.
Ephesians 5:33

Man Up

This is your private prayer journal. Write out the name of one person who made you feel small or like you didn't matter. Then write how that makes you feel now.

Pray Up

Write your own prayer for today. It may be for your wife, kids, or yourself. Whatever God lays on your heart, write it out as a prayer.

Day 17 Prayer

Dear Father,

I pray for our brothers who suffer from the three I's. Brother like to deal in areas of being respected, and capable, but to suddenly find ourselves *Invisible, Irrelevant* or *Isolated* terrifies us.

Father, this usually happens because our shame or hurt causes us to avoid other people. Even family and friends. Lord, this also causes our brothers to avoid You. Men speak and respond to terms of respect, so I pray our brothers will know they are respected when they stand for You.

They may fear being outcasts among their current friends, but eternally, these aren't the friends our brothers need in their lives right now. Lord, I pray for strength and boldness for our brothers who are suffering from one or all three of the I's - *Invisible, Irrelevant* or *Isolated*. I pray they turn to You to be *Seen, Substantial* and *Surrounded*.

Amen

Bro Code Devotional

However, let each one of you love his wife as himself, and let the wife see that she respects her husband.
Ephesians 5:33

76

Brotherly Advice

"If unwilling to rise in the morning, say to thyself, 'I awake to do the work of a man.'"
–Marcus Aurelius

This is your private prayer journal. Are you in the job you want? If so how did you accomplish that. If not, write out why not.

Pray Up

Write your own prayer for today. It may be for your wife, kids, or yourself. Whatever God lays on your heart, write it out as a prayer.

.

Day 18 Prayer

Dear Father,

I pray for a word. Lord, I pray You whisper a word to our brothers who want to follow You, and also brothers who are believers, but have not heard Your voice in a long time. Let them know You are there.

Men are visual and need proof before making big decisions. The disciple, Thomas asked You for evidence, and You were gracious to show him where you were pierced. It didn't make Thomas a bad guy for doubting, it just showed his natural suspicion.

He was in a tough time, just as we are living in tough times. There is so much misinformation about everything that we often don't know where to turn. Who can we trust after all? It's simple—we can trust You.

Please help our brothers get over the hump of not trusting or knowing what to believe. Place Your word in their heart, and allow them to know they were once again touched by Your grace.

Amen

Bro Code Devotional

"Show me what you want me to do. You are my God. Let your good Spirit lead me over level ground."
Psalms 143:10

Man Up

This is your private prayer journal. This is the time for you to write out at least one thing that you need to get off of your chest. Don't pull punches with God, it's time to dig deep and seek His will for your life.

Pray Up

Write your own prayer for today. It may be for your wife, kids, or yourself. Whatever God lays on your heart, write it out as a prayer.

Day 19 Prayer

Dear God,

I pray for our brothers seeking marital purity, but who are stuck with the black mark of unconfessed adultery. One in four husbands cheats on the woman they swore before You to love, honor, and cherish.

Father, there are many reasons why our brothers wander away from the gift You gave them, but help them to know that no excuses are acceptable in Your eyes. Help them to see also that their actions are forgivable sins, but that they must trust You to confess in sincerity and reform.

Only You can change the desires of a willing heart. I pray for this generation of men to stand besides their wife and resist the temptations.

Amen

To preserve you from the evil woman, from the smooth tongue of the adulteress. Do not desire her beauty in your heart, and do not let her capture you with her eyelashes; for the price of a prostitute is only a loaf of bread, but a married woman hunts down a precious life. Can a man carry fire next to his chest and his clothes not be burned? Or can one walk on hot coals and his feet not be scorched? ...

Proverbs 6:24-29

Brotherly Advice

"A man's got to have a code, a creed to live by, no matter his job." –
John Wayne

Man Up

This is your private prayer journal. Write out the name of the last person you felt hatred for. What made so furious, and how did you get over it. You did, didn't you?

Pray Up

Write your own prayer for today. It may be for your wife, kids, or yourself. Whatever God lays on your heart, write it out as a prayer.

Day 20 Prayer

Dear Father,

I pray for our brothers living beneath the dark cloud of shame. We men encounter so much throughout each day that it's easy to do something, whether intentional or not, that brings us into a sin relationship.

This ,of course, separates us from You. Shame is another destructive weapon launched by the devil to tarnish the shine of manhood. Please help our brothers to hold themselves and each other accountable through prayer and confession.

Allow this to help lift the burden of shame we carry. Lift up our brothers and allow them to experience the joy and power of pursuing purity and Your will for their lives. There really is power in the blood.

Amen

But the Lord God helps me; therefore I have not been disgraced; therefore I have set my face like a flint, and I know that I shall not be put to shame.
Isaiah 50:7

Man Up

This is your private prayer journal. Write out what you are most afraid of. Explain where that fear came from and what, if anything, have you done to overcome it.

Pray Up

Write your own prayer for today. It may be for your wife, kids, or yourself. Whatever God lays on your heart, write it out as a prayer.

Lord Father,

Hallelujah that You are the Great Healer. Lord, we as men suffer in silence. We've mistakenly accepted this as a sign of strength, when in fact it's a darkness in our spirits that prevents overcoming past and present hurts.

Father, help our brothers examine their lives and identify past pains that now cause current hurts, anger, or bad actions against themselves or others. Show them that the only way to heal that pain is to bring light to it.

You, Father are that light. Show our brothers to call out to You and confess sins and pray for healing from their wounds. You are the Healer and Redeemer!!

Amen

Fear not, for I am with you; be not dismayed, for I am your God; I will strengthen you, I will help you, I will uphold you with my righteous right hand.
Isaiah 41:10

Brotherly Advice

There is nothing noble being superior to your fellow man; true
nobility is being superior to your former self.
-Winston Churchill

Man Up

This is your private prayer journal. Yep, you guessed it. Its time again for you to write out at least one thing that you need to get off of your chest. Don't pull punches with God, its time to dig deep and seek His will for your life.

Pray Up

Write your own prayer for today. It may be for your wife, kids, or yourself. Whatever God lays on your heart, write it out as a prayer.

Dear Father,

I pray for brothers struggling with one or more of the 3 A's. Too often, we fail at Adultery, Addiction, or Anger. I pray for our brothers who are seeking a way out of the devil's tactics.

So often, any of these A's are rooted in pain from our brothers' pasts. So often, our childhood or parents left wounds on our souls that have never healed. These injuries can lead to adultery, addiction, and anger.

Father, show these brothers it is okay to open up and seek healing. Getting better is not a sign of weakness. It is a great strength. Please show them the hurt they cause others because they hurt inside too. This isn't a prayer for the weak, my Lord.

This is a plea for strong, respectable men to feel the value of self-worth and being healed from their past, so they will stop hurting the ones they love with the 3 A's.

Amen

Bro Code Devotional

*He will wipe away every tear from their eyes, and death shall be no more,
neither shall there be mourning, nor crying, nor pain anymore, for the
former things have passed away."*
Revelation 21:4

Man Up

This is your private prayer journal. If you are married , write a prayer for your wife. If not, pray for someone significant in your life.

Pray Up

Write your own prayer for today. It may be for your wife, kids, or yourself. Whatever God lays on your heart, write it out as a prayer.

Lord,
I pray for our brothers who are blessed to be married. I ask that You inspire them to pursue marital purity. You created marriage to reflect our relationship with You.

Because You are the gift giver, the way we treat our wife reflects not only on us men, but on how we love You. Father, marital purity is not a subject often discussed among men.

The crude locker room chatter still prevails in and outside of the room. I pray our brothers open their hearts to the destruction of those words, and consider speaking of their wife and any woman with respect.

Lord, I pray that if anyone is considering infidelity that they would flee from temptation. Show them that's it's not the coward who runs, but the dead who tempt the powerful enemy of sexual sin.

Amen

Bro Code Devotional

No temptation has overtaken you that is not common to man. God is faithful, and he will not let you be tempted beyond your ability, but with the temptation he will also provide the way of escape, that you may be able to endure it.
1 Corinthians 10:13

Brotherly Advice

It takes a great man to be a good listener.
-Calvin Coolidge

This is your private prayer journal. How has your attitude about doing these 31 days of prayers changed from the first day you began your challenge?

Pray Up

Write your own prayer for today. It may be for your wife, kids, or yourself. Whatever God lays on your heart, write it out as a prayer.

Day 24 Prayer

Dear Lord,

Praise You for family. Thank You for our parents and siblings. Father, we know not every family unit is supportive, caring or in tact, but that doesn't prohibit the need to honor our mother and father.

Your word says nothing about judging our earthly parents, but that we are to honor them. I pray that if there is pain associated with a brother's family, that the model of honoring despite the injuries will allow them to follow Your example as being a Godly father to their kids so that the cycle of family dysfunction and strife ends at their generation.

Father, You are a good, good Father. We men can do better through You. I pray that Your heart for family will shine through to brothers still in the struggle to be the head of their household.

Amen

But I want you to understand that the head of every man is Christ, the head of a wife is her husband, and the head of Christ is God
1 Corinthians 11:3

Man Up

This is your private prayer journal. If God came back at this very moment, where would you go? Explain why you feel that way.

Pray Up

Write your own prayer for today. It may be for your wife, kids, or yourself. Whatever God lays on your heart, write it out as a prayer.

Day 25 Prayer

Holy Father,

I pray that You show our brothers fighting the pull of pornography that there is a way out of their sexual bondage. Let them sincerely understand the damage they do to themselves and those around them by succumbing to the temptation of sexual sin.

Father, the secrets, the lies, and the deception associated with sexual sin are the chains used by the devil to lock men down into the bowels of hell. Men cannot overcome satan without Your mighty authority.

Help them to seek the resources to lead them into a life changing decision to break those shackles. I pray, Father, that they will seek other brothers to hold them accountable and that they not be stopped by shame or guilt, but that they seek freedom through faith and confession.

Amen

But I say, walk by the Spirit, and you will not gratify the desires of the flesh.
Galatians 5:16

Brotherly Advice

A man does what he must -- in spite of personal consequences, in spite of obstacles and dangers, and pressures -- and that is the basis of all human morality.

-John Kennedy

Man Up

This is your private prayer journal. Do you need to forgive your dad? If so, what has he done or not done in your life that hurt you? What would you say to him.

Pray Up

Write your own prayer for today. It may be for your wife, kids, or yourself. Whatever God lays on your heart, write it out as a prayer.

Day 26 Prayer

Lord God,

I pray that Your merciful hand lay down upon our brothers who are struggling to labor. Brothers who are out of work or who have lost the joy in the work they do.

Work is fulfilling for a man, and You bless the fruitful with more abundance than their efforts may produce. Lord, I ask Your grace for our brothers fighting to provide for their family, even if there doesn't seem to be a way.

Show them the path. Our brothers equate work with providing, and being able to provide with respect. This causes so much stress and worry for men. It chips away at their true joy. I pray they may know peace in their labor and take the time to relax while with their family.

Amen

Whatever you do, work heartily, as for the Lord and not for men, knowing that from the Lord you will receive the inheritance as your reward. You are serving the Lord Christ.
Colossians 3:23-24

Man Up

This is your private prayer journal. Write out three things that staring today, you can become better about. Then explain how you will go about being better.

Pray Up

Write your own prayer for today. It may be for your wife, kids, or yourself. Whatever God lays on your heart, write it out as a prayer.

Day 27 Prayer

Lord God,

Place Your hand upon your army of men. Help us to heal from the pain of past hurts. We think by building a hard shell around our emotional man, that we are protected from attacks and injuries.

While the natural man may learn to endure the storms, it is the spirit man that withers within these walls. Not showing emotional vulnerability or allowing anyone to get close is a sure path to destruction and regret.

Show us that the hard shell we construct doesn't protect us from injury, it actually helps seal the hurts inside. Lord, help us to break the bricks that prevent us from healing.

Amen

But he gives more grace. Therefore it says, "God opposes the proud, but gives grace to the humble."
James 4:6

Brotherly Advice

Men are like steel. When they lose their temper, they lose their
worth.
-Chuck Norris

Man Up

This is your private prayer journal. Write out how you would feel if someone stole something from you. What would you do to get it back and what would you do to that person?

Pray Up

Write your own prayer for today. It may be for your wife, kids, or yourself. Whatever God lays on your heart, write it out as a prayer.

Day 28 Prayer

Dear Father,

I pray that You show our brothers the power of prayer. I ask that they read Your word in 1 John 5:14-15 and have the boldness to ask and the confidence to expect their prayers to become one with Your will.

Lord, show our brothers how to pray with expectancy, but also show them first how to clear the path of sin debris that blocks the direct communication with you. Too many believers toil in vein over prayers that will not be answered.

Not because You don't love them, but because unconfessed sin and unrepentant hearts interfere with the intimacy You seek. I pray they come into a close and constant conversation with their loving Father, who is so willing to answer their petitions.

Amen

"And this is the confidence that we have toward him, that if we ask anything according to his will he hears us. And if we know that he hears us in whatever we ask, we know that we have the requests that we have asked of him."
1 John 5:14-15

Man Up

This is your private prayer journal. Are you the biblical man of the house? If so, explain why you feel that way. If not, what will you do to improve.

Pray Up

Write your own prayer for today. It may be for your wife, kids, or yourself. Whatever God lays on your heart, write it out as a prayer.

Dear Lord,

Help our brothers to remain all in with their family. Encourage brothers to engage with their wife and kids when they are together. To be the man that You created them to be.

Holy, righteous, bold and loving. Our families need us to lead the team. Switch off the TV or internet, and allow those who love you and look up to you, and get to know you.

Putting your phone down will open up incredible streams of communications with family and other believers. Father, you ordained men to be the mirror of You.

You made us so perfectly in Your image so our kids can learn about You through their mom and dads. Lord the only way for others to see the Christ in them is to go all in with their time, attention, love and focus on the family.

Amen

Then God said, "Let Us make man in Our image, according to Our likeness; and let them rule over the fish of the sea and over the birds of the sky and over the cattle and over all the earth, and over every creeping thing that creeps on the earth." So God created mankind in his own image, in the image of God he created them; male and female he created them.

Genesis 1:26-27

Brotherly Advice

It is not titles that make men illustrious, but men who make titles illustrious.
-Machiavelli

Man Up

This is your private prayer journal. Write you what you understand a God-centered life looks like.

Pray Up

Write your own prayer for today. It may be for your wife, kids, or yourself. Whatever God lays on your heart, write it out as a prayer.

Day 30 Prayer

Lord God,

I pray for peace for my brothers. You know their struggles. They may be with finances, addiction, adultery, depression, or self-doubt. You know they are NOT broken, but wounded.

Help them to commit their troubles to You and leave them at the foot of the cross for You to address. Father, so often we men avoid looking back out of fear of what we might see. The past is never as far away as we would like to think.

It's within that past that so much pain was caused and created. Men prefer to forge ahead, when in reality instead of leaving our troubles behind, we are just dragging them along.

God, grant our brothers the courage to see what has really caused them pain, whether it was in their past or right in their face, allow them to seek Your healing.

Amen

Bro Code Devotional

"You shall not worship them or serve them; for I, the LORD your God, am a jealous God, visiting the iniquity of the fathers on the children, on the third and the fourth generations of those who hate Me.

Exodus 20:5

Man Up

This is your private prayer journal. What makes you feel unworthy or unwanted. Explain what those factors influence you in that way, and what will you do to change.

Pray Up

Write your own prayer for today. It may be for your wife, kids, or yourself. Whatever God lays on your heart, write it out as a prayer.

Day 31 Prayer

Dear Father,

Hallelujah for these last 31 days. You have spoken life, love respect and healing our men. They are so precious to You and respected within the kingdom.

Father, these last generations have attacked men for being men. Their power and masculinity has been insulted with efforts by the devil to corrode and water down what Your word describes as manhood.

I am so thankful that You allowed this prayer book to become reality and pray it has been a blessing. I pray that each section has been filled out by a beloved brother. If they didn't have time to search their soul during the prayers, I ask they take the time very soon and write, think, or pray through their relationship with You.

God, I pray this brother comes to know You in a deeper way than they've ever imagined.

Amen

"For the Lord God is a sun and shield; the Lord bestows favor and honor; no good thing does He withhold from those who walk uprightly."
Psalm 84:11

Brotherly Advice

Big jobs usually go to the men who prove their ability to outgrow
small ones.

-Theodore Roosevelt

This is your private prayer journal. Write out your personal testimony. And then pat yourself on the back for rocking out a 31 day prayer challenge. Great going!

Pray Up

Write your own prayer for today. It may be for your wife, kids, or yourself. Whatever God lays on your heart, write it out as a prayer.

Preview - Bro, Man Up

Available Now

Bro, Man Up

I'd like to start this off with a promise. I'm not going to bore you with another feel-good, pat-on-the-back book that gets tossed onto your wife's nightstand. I don't read them either. This is a conversation between you and me.

I wrote this for men, my Bros, in hopes of encouraging you to embrace your alpha manhood without having to worry about being attacked for it.

Now, the truth is, we can do better. In some cases, much better, but until we know where we've been, there's no way we'll ever know where we're going. Can we continue to crawl through the same daily grind?

Sure, and we might just reach the grand old age of average life expectancy. But would you rather steal home base with a scorching headfirst dive while avoiding a brick wall catcher, or stroll across the plate because the pitcher walked a batter on loaded bases?

Honestly, if the latter is your choice, the Bro Code Series might not be for you. Nah, I'm kidding, but what does matter is that we round the bases and finish this gift called life stronger than we began.

I say life is a gift because that's a theme you'll see throughout this quick hitter.

God gave us this life, and it is a precious gift, and no matter what society, your family or even your friends may say, you are an amazing gift because God created you to be so.

I know most of us have treated our gift as if it were a little brother's birthday present, but when you think back to all of the stupid stuff we did, and how lucky we are to be alive, it really is amazing to be here at all.

So, since we're here at this moment together, how about we give this a look and see what's going on about this business of manhood.

Bro Code Goal

There's so much static these days about men, but I'm going to cut through the fog and not worry about being PC (politically correct) or stepping on toes. I can apologize later if that's what it takes to keep you in the game, but for now, let's set some ground rules for getting through the Bro Code Series.

The purpose, goal and intention is to encourage you to build the better man. Not that you aren't freaking incredible the way you are, but let's be honest, if there weren't at least a few rough edges in your life, you wouldn't be reading this.

And, if the Bro Code Series was given to you by someone as a "gift," then maybe you haven't noticed how rough your patches are. As for me, I'm still sanding down rough spots, and working to be that better man, so there's zero judgment among Bros. This is more like teamwork than telling you what to do. We men are stronger together anyways, right?

And if one prevail against him, two shall withstand him; and a threefold cord is not quickly broken.
Ecclesiastes 4:12

The scope is simple. How do we go about building the better man?

Before we start twisting wrenches and sparking up the torch out in the man cave, I want to throw another truth at you. I like to offer men what I call "bailouts." Those are opportunities when you're really not digging a tough situation, so you get to exit without feeling bad about being at the right place for the wrong reason.

It's like getting up and going to the bathroom in church. It's awkward, so you just hold on, but you're miserable. Now, if they offered a bailout by turning off the lights or something, then there'd be an exodus to the potty like kindergarteners after lunch.

The bailouts I'll offer along the way of this book are when I know we're approaching a crossroads that'll require making a decision one way or the other. I'm not saying there aren't other options of building the better man, but there is only one way of becoming him. And let's be honest, not every man is going to want to improve.

Some Bros are happy to wake up and see that there's not a police chalk line drawn around their body. They figure that they've lucked out another day, so why not get up and see what happens while they're awake.

There is so much more to life than merely getting by. We were created to be rulers, conquerors, kings and priests. It's in God's holy Word. Oh by the way, everything I'm going to share with you is based on His Word.

After all, who would you rather trust for ageless, sage advice: me or the big guy? But, in the event that you didn't see the writing on the wall, you could bail out now if you're totally averse to my leaning on God's Word to hang out with you.

Still here? Awesome, and God bless you, Bro. Building the better man is certainly subjective as to the condition of "better," so we're going to focus on the spirit-man as much as the natural-man. While the earthly definitions are as varied as the Bros reading this book series, there's a pretty consistent standard for living life as a godly man.

Setting our face toward God allows us to know His ultimate goal for why He created us in the first place. This in turn will help us chart our own paths toward an incredible life of victory. I like this brief and to the point verse from Colossians 3:2:

Set your minds on things above, not on earthly things.

Bro Truth and Consequences

Ever wonder why this was all created in the first place? When I began thinking bigger and allowing my mind to roam beyond yesterday's sports scores, it soon became uncomfortable, so I stopped. I limited myself and my awareness to just what was within my grasp. Like whatever is on the middle shelf in your fridge: it's easy, so we go for it. But we miss out on the opportunity to have enjoyed something much better with only a little effort to look past the expired milk.

I recall many decades ago while in college, sitting on a porch step with my girlfriend at the time. I was in my freshman year minoring in psychology, so I assumed I had a depth of universal knowledge that would immediately impress her. Actually, I just figured I'd blow her mind with my nineteen-year-old wisdom gained from sandlot football and Saturday morning cartoons.

The truth is, as we stared up into an endless, star-speckled opportunity to understand what it was we were mindlessly looking at or looking for, I had zero idea what I was saying. I wasn't even sure if she was listening, but it really didn't matter until she asked the one question that every deep-thinking Bro has pondered. No, not that.

She asked, "What's the meaning of it all?"

I catalogued my best 1980s MTV music lyrics (yes, this was in the 80s) and my mind drew a blank. I was going to recite a line or two from someone like John Cougar Mellencamp or Cyndi Lauper. But the bigness of her question and the smallness of my testosterone-driven mind caused me to waffle within the potential for delivering a life-changing response.

"Love," I finally whispered.

She smiled and I saw the twinkle in her eye. Yes, she agreed that it was indeed all about love. I exhaled off to the side because I knew I'd just dodged a bullet, and had also potentially made a little headway with her. And just like that, her dad walked out onto the porch and said those fateful words that I'll never forget.

"Go home, Scott. You're drunk."

You know the worst part about that night so long ago, besides being immediately humiliated after delivering such an amazing pickup line to an incredible-looking girl? Her dad was right. I was drunk, and I was extremely shallow in my emotional understanding of anything beyond having a good time at everyone else's expense. So why share that swing and miss?

When I began writing the Bro Code Series I started out with a first draft, and then many more to follow until someone finally said I had to stop rewriting the opening sentence over and over again. But in those early attempts I was going to roll out my resume on a regal red carpet and allow you the time to be royally impressed. Not that I was expecting you to applaud loudly and call out my name as you set a personal record in your latest CrossFit competition, but I wouldn't stop you if you had chosen to do so.

Instead, I knew it was best to begin with the very same thing we'll end with, and that is the truth. I think we connect best when we stop measuring macho co..., *socks* and instead accept each other as we are. I wanted to share the truth about my life in hopes that you'll find connection points that help you to say, "You too, Bro?"

Yes, me too, Bro, and so many other men who want to do better but might not know how to do better. Within the layers of what makes us who we are, there is a physical body, a soul and a spirit. Most of my life I abused my body, numbed my soul and denied my spirit. Sure, I tried to cover up what was empty inside with a laundry list of accomplishments, but in the end, just like on the porch that fateful summer night, I had nothing inside.

Once we men commit to dropping the tattered bags holding our busted trophies and dog-eared certificates, and seek God's purpose, then we'll understand His desire for our lives. It all starts with Him, and in this truth I'll share why we are here. You see, although I was young, dumb and full of Keystone Light at the time, I was actually right when I slurred out the word, "Love."

Of course, her dad knew that the love I was talking about had nothing to do with Jesus and everything to do with the daughter he wasn't going to lose to some poacher passed out on his front porch.

It was in love that we were created for relationship. God created us to glorify Him, and that's why we were made in His image. We are not some single-cell organism that belly-crawled from prehistoric goo (bailout alert on anti-evolutionism) to evolve over millions of years into the studly Bros that we are today. God created us to be perfect like Him, and He did it out of love.

Check out Genesis 1:26 where God the Father is talking with Jesus the Son and the Holy Spirit about you and me.

Then God said, "Let us make mankind in our image, in our likeness, so that they may rule over the fish in the sea and the birds in the sky, over the livestock and all the wild animals, and over all the creatures that move along the ground."

I underlined a few cool points in this very important scripture. I'm not going to assume you do or don't dig into the bible. Honestly, the men who get so wrapped up in their own religious interpretation of what God is trying to lay out are the ones I avoid. But I do want to keep it straight and accurate for the sake of laying down this foundational principle to better man building.

You are not an accident. You were purposefully created by an intentional act of God. When He says "let us" and "in our," He is talking about the Trinity, which is God the Father, Christ the Son and the Holy Spirit. Remember earlier when I said we were intended to be rulers, conquerors, kings and priests? Here is the very first mention of what we were placed on this earth to do—"*that they rule over...*"

That scripture is truth. There is no way of getting around it or denying it. So if you're still on the fence about evolution of the species, then it's an argument you'll have to take up with God. Otherwise, it's pretty clear, my Brother ruler of everything, that we were created in God's image for a very special purpose.

Now you may be asking, "But what happened?"

Consequences are what happened. There are consequences for sin, and one of the most serious is described in Romans 6, and is death.

For the wages of sin is death, but the gift of God is eternal life in Christ Jesus our Lord.
Romans 6:23

Although physical death is surely a possibility, the death referenced in Romans is exactly the death experienced by Adam and Eve when they sinned in the garden of Eden. Death is separation from God. You see, Bro, when we sin, there are consequences. In those unconfessed consequences, we are doomed to scraping through a life alone and absent of God. Now you might say that's no big deal, but compare the blessed life of favor enjoyed by Adam in the garden and the life of hardship he suffered once exiled.

So how did we go from being God's right-hand Bro to getting kicked out and spawning generations of broken Brothers? It was sin and its consequence of death. Of course, God never closes one door without opening another. In that second door is what the bible refers to as the Second Adam. Not another failed natural-man, but a glorious victor in the spirit-man of Jesus Christ.

Looking at this from another angle, "bearing fruit" is a cool expression through the bible, and one that we should take time to meditate over. It starts with sowing and reaping. Let's say you eat junk food (sowing), then what you will get is fat (reaping). Same thing in the construction process of building the better man. If we cut corners, cheat and look for the easy way out, we'll suffer the consequences and won't have the personal foundation to sustain success.

If you believe in God, and there have been several bailout opportunities long before this point to stop reading the Bro Code Series, so I'll assume you do, this is critical to success as a godly Bro.

Wow that was a crazy long, run-on sentence. Point is, there is no straddling the fence with faith. Either you are all in on your belief that God is real, or you aren't. There is no neutral ground. I know you're invested in living the blessed life.

God doesn't lie, tease, give false hope or waste eternal efforts trying to jerk you around. What He says, He means. If it doesn't become real, it's because of your jacked-up process of sowing and reaping.

Read this promise and tell me what you think God is saying to you. I'm serious about this; take your time. Break it down. Allow it to speak to you. Proclaim the promises. Willingly accept God's blessings.

This is power packed, so please absorb every word. This is your life after all, and I want you to live it like the alpha male God created you to be!

I am the vine; you are the branches. If you remain in me and I in you, you will bear much fruit; apart from me you can do nothing. If you do not remain in me, you are like a branch that is thrown away and withers; such branches are picked up, thrown into the fire and burned. If you remain in me and my words remain in you, ask whatever you wish, and it will be done for you. This is to my Father's glory, that you bear much fruit, showing yourselves to be my disciples.
John 15:5-8

You see, I may have suffered the consequences of being a slobbering drunk muscle-head in college, but God allowed me a second chance through the spirit-man as reflected in Christ. And when I proudly guessed at the word love for my soon-to-be-never-seen-again, I was unwittingly correct. It is all about love. It's about God's love for us and not only that He created us, but also why He created us.

Why Are We Here?

Have you ever taken the time to ask what's it all about? Between the hustle of life and the bustle of trying to make your way within its stream, there are times when we question our purpose. I'd imagine the answer is like mine in that we've got way too much stuff to do to sit around worrying about the why.

The irony is that the core of the question, "why?" is simple, yet it's either avoided or misunderstood.

God created us with a purpose... That purpose is to glorify Him. Now, I can see where some might take this to mean that God was selfish because He created for himself His own little cheerleading squad: "Go God!!!"

...everyone who is called by my name, whom I created for my glory, whom
I formed and made.
Isaiah 43:7

The truth is that God did not need us. He doesn't have an ego to pump or people to high-five. When you look back over the course of human history, we've pretty much made a mess of things. So, when the bible says to glorify Him, it is only out of His love that we were created, and for love that we remain. We were created out of God, so in us is a piece of Him. Because He is love, then we too are a reflection of that love.

Did that paragraph make you want to grab the man card out of my hand and thrash it into a heap of scraps? I can understand that, because I would've wanted to do the same thing at one point in my life. What changed? I learned that I didn't have to be so hard in my life to be tough. I was a man who never showed emotion, and I never cut myself slack in anything—ever. When I came to understand what it was to build the better man, I realized that the capacity to give and receive love was the key.

I'm going to pound on my chest for a bit. I might not have known it back then, and her dad sure didn't appreciate me when I said it, but love was the right answer after all. Too bad I was too blind to see the truth, although I did suffer the consequences.

I give all glory and praise to my heavenly Father. It was His son, Jesus Christ who lifted me up when I wanted to stay down, and the Holy Spirit who now pours life into my soul so that I may pour out into others.

I want to thank my loving *ezer*, Leah and our wonderfully blended family of kids and a French Bulldog named, Bacon.

A special appreciation to my editors, Imogen Howson and Kim Cannon, along with the best cover artist ever, Darlene Albert of Wicked Smart Design.

About the Author

Scott is a son of the Living God. He's thankful for the gift of his wife, Leah. They have seven kids combined.

Scott was career law enforcement until God called him into His service in 2015. He promptly retired as a Chief of Police and started the Blue Marriage ministry with Leah.

The "Chief" admits what he thought he'd learned from leading others during a 25 year career that included 12 years undercover and 16 years in SWAT, was nothing like leading people to Christ.

Scott is currently in seminary at The King's University's Doctor of Ministry program. He's also earned a Master of Public Administration and a Ph.D. in Cultural Anthropology.

In 2016, he was led to start the Brick Breakers Men's Ministry with the mission of encouraging other alpha males like him, who've suffered in silence, and found themselves in a society that is increasing the pressures to abandon God's principles of manhood as found in this life-guiding verse.

Be on your guard; stand firm in the faith; be courageous; be strong. Do everything in love.
1 Corinthians 16:13-14

Scott serves on the team at MarriageToday as the director of content development, and publishing. He and Leah love the Lord and the passion He's placed on their hearts for divorced people, remarried couples and blended families.

An experienced mentor and confidential accountability partner, please contact Scott if he can help you personally, or speak with your church, group or conference.

Mission Checklist:

- Watch your other Bros' 6!
    - Share The Bro Code Series with men.
    - Leave a review online wherever you bought this book.
    - Post the book and buy links on your social media so others find the help they need.
    - Message me for interviews, speaking, blog tour or questions.
    - **Be the Bro that God created you to be!**

ALSO BY SCOTT SILVERII

THE BRO CODE SERIES

Bro, Man Up

Bro, Keep It In Your Pants

Bro, You Free?

Bro, Stay Free

Broken and Blue

A Darker Shade of Blue

Cop Culture: Why Good Cops Go Bad

31 Days of Prayer for Men

The ABCs of Marriage

31 Days of Prayer for a Cop

Made in the USA
Monee, IL
17 December 2020